My inspiration..........

This book is dedicated to a few people. Their names are James Anthony, James Nehemiah, and Gabriela Alexis. I dedicate this to Gabby and Nehemiah (my babies), because it was through the carrying of them, that I gained my strength. I dedicate this to my husband, James Anthony, because he has been my support through it all. I love yall, and I always strive to make yall smile☺

Ashes No More

The Birthing of Greatness

How I came to be......

1 John 4:19

We love because God first loved us.

Sometimes we see people and we never know the story behind their smile. I've never known a person to have a perfect life, but for some reason, in the church we seem to look at certain people that have certain titles in a specific light as if to say that they never had to struggle in life. That is definitely not the testimony of many sincere leaders in ministry. There is always a journey that has been traveled, some harder or longer than others. Me being the wife of a pastor, it took me a long time to come to terms with the fact that my life had actually happened the way that it did. Some things I had decided to block out of my memory years ago, while others I had to live with daily. Throughout my life, there were days that I still can't believe I conquered.

Ashes No More

There were years of confusion and distrust. My testimony is simply that, the foundation upon which I have grown.

On January 17th, 1988, Andre and Cynthia Williams became one in the sight of God. On October 18, 1988, Chaun'Dela Tomieka Williams was born. After having me, my parents moved to New York. I am not sure how long we were there, but I do know that we were not there for a long time. Some things happened between my mother and father, and my mother then decided to go back home to South Carolina. From what I have been told, my father simply had an addiction that he did not want to let go of. What I do remember is my father coming to South Carolina while we lived in a little small apartment in Saint Stephen, South Carolina. I am not sure how old I was when he came, but I do remember the day he left, like it was yesterday. We had one of those sofas with the wooden frame. The cushions were black and brown. My mom used to take a cushion off and put it on the floor for me to sit on when it was time for me to get my hair done. On this particular day, I was getting my hair done, and my dad came in the living room with a long black trench coat on and some grey pants. I am not sure what color his shirt was, but I do remember the crease in his pants. He stood in front of me and said "Alright y'all, I'll be right back." No hug, no kiss, nothing….and just like that…he was gone.

Ashes No More

My mother, on the other hand, was a very strong woman. She basically supported me by herself for the first 5 years of my life. When I was a baby, my mother and father separated, and we moved in with my grandparents. Her and my grandparents were the most important people in my life. My mother worked a lot of nights in a nursing home when I was younger, so I spent many of nights at home with my grandparents. I was known as their "tugga", a name that will forever stay in my heart.

My earliest happy memories are with my grandmother. I remember her dark brown skin and her pretty brown eyes. She had a wig for just about every day of the week, and I don't remember seeing her without one very often. She was a very petite lady. I still remember her smell like it was yesterday. It was a mixture of rubbing alcohol (because she used that for everything) and the perfumes that she would use. I remember sitting in the kitchen and getting my hair straightened by the gas stove. I even remember sitting at the table eating flour with her. Yes, my grandmother and I would sit at the kitchen table with two spoons and eat flour together. She was an amazing woman!

One of the main things that I remember was the fact that she and my mother kept me in church all the time. My grandmother was a part of a very small church, where the Pastor was also her best friend. My grandmother was the church mother, and she definitely lived up to her title. She was even the mother of the community. She was the one that all the neighborhood children came to buy little snacks. I remember everyone used to call her "Aunt Evelina". She sold, pickled eggs, pickled pigs feet, hotdogs, hot sausages, and "chili bears". Our house always had people coming in and out asking for credit so that they could get things for free. I loved every minute of it.

Another thing that I remember about my grandmother was her wardrobe! My grandmother was one of the most colorful people that I have ever encountered. She also believed in wearing a hat with just about every outfit. I remember looking in her closet and wondering what went with what. The prints that I remember seeing the most are flowers and polka dots. My grandmother believed in hats with every outfit, and she had boots galore. She was definitely a person with her own sense of style.

She was also a good wife. I remember eating a home cooked meal just about every day. I don't really have any memories of eating fast food or even spending a lot of money when I was younger. My grandmother cooked and cleaned every day. She even got up every morning and got my grandfather's lunch together for him before he went to work. She was a lady by her own right. I will always love and remember her.

Ashes No More

My grandfather, on the other hand, was one man unlike any other in my life. His name was James Adams, but he went by the name Adam. He had to quit school at a very early age to help his mother take care of the family, so he never really knew how to read. He also had been in a bad accident when he was younger, which left him with one arm. Some people might wonder why I would put that in here, but that played a big part in who he was and my relationship with him. Now, I will say that didn't stop him from doing anything that he put his mind to. He was a hard worker for as long as I could remember. And there was definitely never a dull moment. Because he only had one arm, he was the first person to ever let me hold the steering wheel. When he would try to move his mirrors or even get his chewing tobacco out of the packet, he would say "Tooga, hold the wheel". I loved it!

My grandparents taught me soooo much growing up. Of all of those lessons, I learned that family was the foundation for the fruit of life.

My grandmother passed away when I was in the second grade, and it still feels like yesterday. She had a stroke, and never fully recovered from it. That was one of the hardest struggles that I ever went through. Let me explain why.

My mother was not raised by her birth parents. So, the loving people that I knew to be my grandparents weren't my biological grandparents.

Ashes No More

My grandmother was on drugs and my grandfather wasn't around, so they were relatives of my grandmother that took my mother in. That being said, she had other children, and when she got sick, they moved her in with them. The day before she had a stroke is the last time that I remember seeing her. And to be honest, I would rather remember her that way. When her children took her, I just remember there being a lot of animosity and unreleased pain between my mother and her children. My mother and I even went to see her one night while she was recovering at her daughter's house, and they wouldn't let us see her. When she died, I remember going to the funeral and sitting in the back. They didn't even put our names on the obituary. This was a lady that I slept in the bed with all my life, up until she got sick. I can still see the tears in my mother's eyes looking at the casket from the back of the church. We didn't even get to sit in a pew, we had to sit in some of the extra chairs that they lined up against the wall when they ran out of room. Her children really did change a lot of things. I don't even remember my grandfather being at the funeral. That was the first time that my heart was broken. Sitting in the back of that church, I could still hear her telling me that she loved me, and wrapping her arms around me. She was unbelievable woman that could never be replaced in my life.

Ashes No More

As time went by, my grandfather was forced to move out of the house that he built with my grandmother, and he had to move into a trailer in another town. Let's just say that life was very different after that.

My mother and I then moved into a house by ourselves. It was different, but it was what we had to do at the time. She had been dating a gentleman, and they were beginning to get very serious, so I knew it would only be a matter of time before they got married.

After they got married, we moved into a house that his family owned around the corner from the house that I grew up in with my grandparents. I really couldn't stand that house. It was a very old house that sat almost in the middle of the woods. It only had two bedrooms, and you could stand in the living room and see every single room. The floors squeaked with every step that we took. There was definitely no sneaking up on anyone there. It was a very dark house. I don't remember having much sunlight shining in.

There were also memories in that house that made it a lot darker than it probably was to the natural eye. The clearest memory that I had in that house was on a Sunday afternoon. We had just come home from our first service, and my mother was on her way to another service in Goose Creek, SC. She told me to get dressed, but I didn't listen. I remember her telling me that if I wasn't ready by the time she picked up her keys, then she was going to leave me at home. I still didn't listen. When I heard her pick up her keys, I ran and tried to get dressed fast enough to go with her. I heard the truck engine start, and slipped on my shoes. I was wearing a peach and white flowery dress with a bow that tied in the back with shiny white shoes and ruffled socks. By the time I got to the door, she was pulling out of the yard. I literally ran down the road behind the car crying and yelling for her to stop, but she kept driving. When I got back to the house, I was still crying. The person that she left me with was sitting on the loveseat right in front of the front door. I was crying, so he told me to come sit by him. At this point I trusted him. Not because I knew him, but simply because my mother had trusted him enough to leave me with him. When I sat on his lap, he told me that it was going to be ok, and that my mother was going to be right back. He put me in his lap, and spoke gently for me to stop crying. His voice was almost like a whisper. Once I calmed down, he hugged me and told me that it was ok. I then remember him rubbing my left knee in a circular motion. At the age of 7, it seemed innocent enough. I then remember him sliding his hands up my dress and touching me in a way that was very uncomfortable and repeating the words "It's Okay".

When my mother got home, I said nothing.

Ashes No More

Let's fast forward a little over a year later. My mother is working nights at this time. I am left with the same person that I was left with before. At this time, I am not thinking about the things that happened before, because it has been so long. He is in another room watching wrestling. I am laying on the couch in the living room watching the news. I start to doze off. Even though this was so long ago, I can still remember hearing him walk into the living room. The floors were squeaking so loudly that it sounded like they were screaming out for me. Even then, I had an eerie feeling. It's like I went completely numb before he could even get to me. Deep down in my stomach, I knew what was going to happen. I just laid there. I was laying on the couch on my stomach. My eyes were closed. I tried to imagine myself someplace else...anyplace other than that couch. I could feel him standing next to the chair for a minute....almost like he wanted to make sure that I was asleep. At that very moment, I just wanted to jump up and run away. He came and sat at the foot of the chair. I had on some blue shorts and a white shirt. I felt his hands on my calves. They then moved up to that same place, and again came that feeling of uncomfort. I remember tears falling down my cheeks while he had his way with me. I felt at that moment that I was alone in the world. I just couldn't come up with a reason as to what I could have done to deserve this. I will never forget thinking that I

Ashes No More

was being punished. At such a young age, I did not know what was happening to me, but I did know that it wasn't right. I knew that for some reason it made me feel dirty. It made me feel punished.

This time I spoke up!!!

Telling my mother was by far one of the hardest things that I have ever had to do. Before telling her, I felt like my world was going to come to an end. I even sat in my room and practiced telling her. I cried for at least an hour before she came home from work, because I was so afraid of what her reaction would be. I felt like my stomach was going to turn inside out....I felt weak just thinking about her reaction.

When she came home, I remember telling her that I needed to talk to her. Of course, the person was there, as well. I asked if I could talk to her alone, and she simply told me to say what I had to say. The fact that he denied it....that was to be expected. The fact that my mother believed him wasn't........

That was the day I lost trust in men and stopped believing in the power of my words.....

After that day, I simply began to internalize my feelings. My stepfather had a cousin that was around the same age as me. We grew up almost like sisters. Their grandmother was the Pastor of the church, so I was always used to being around

Ashes No More

them anyway. On Sundays she and I would fight over who would get to play the drums and who would get to play the tambourine that had all the pieces to it. Everyone always thought that we were sisters instead of cousins, because we were always together. We would even go in her room after services and play shouting music so that we could practice our shouting and mimic the people that we had seen in prior services. Those memories will be in my heart forever.

Now, I am not going to go into detail with everything that happened to me growing up, because this would end up becoming a never ending story. I just want to set a foundation.

Now, when I say this, I pray that no one gets offended.

Being that my mother worked all the time because she was a single parent, as I stated before, I spent most of my time with my grandparents. There were no issues with my mother, I simply spent more time with them. She was never on drugs, she didn't abandon me, she simply had to provide to me, and she was blessed enough to have a great support system that didn't mind stepping in to help her when she needed it the most.

That being said, when my mother got married and we officially moved out on our on, it was somewhat of an adjustment for me. I slept in the same bed with my grandmother up until she got sick....that alone should speak volumes. I had to get used to the fact that not only was my grandmother no longer with me, but I was going to have to get used to sharing my mother, as well. So, growing up....there definitely were times when I wanted to have my mother to myself. I didn't understand why then, but as I got older I realized that it was simply because I never got to have her with no interruptions. Little did I know, it would still work out for my good.

Something wonderful did come out of everything, though. I was able to spend a lot of time with my godparents/cousins. They were foster parents, so they always had other kids and teenagers around. They were definitely a blessing to me. My godfather was a man a view words....at times. I remember him sitting at the head of the kitchen table with his bible open, reading quietly. Everyone would try to walk by him quickly, so he wouldn't stop them. The thing was, you had to walk by him to get something to eat, go to the bathroom, get to the trashcan, or even get to the laundry room. But, he would always manage to catch me. At the time, because I was young, I didn't cherish and understand those moments the way that I do, now. He was definitely a male role model that I will never forget. And even though it seemed like him and my godmother never got to spend any time together alone, they showed me firsthand what sacrificial love was.

Ashes No More

They sacrificed for others all of the time, but yet, she would not let anyone come in her house and disrespect her OR her husband. I have seen many children have to leave her house, simply because they talked to her husband the wrong way.

They took me in when I felt like I didn't have a place to go in this world. My mother was still a part of my life. She didn't hand me over to them. I just wanted to be around other children with other issues. I was an only child, and sometimes I felt like I was just lonely. Some people may not have understood why I was there all of the time, but I would like to clarify and set the record straight. I wasn't unhappy at home. I just wanted to be around people. My mother worked a lot, and I didn't want to be home with myself. I didn't understand why then, but now I see that I just didn't want to deal with thoughts and memories. I didn't want to deal with my issues.

Romans 5:3

We also boast in our troubles, because we know that trouble produces endurance.

To Every Action- There is a Reaction

My Teenage Years

Psalm 126:5

They who sow in tears shall reap in joy and singing.

After many years of trying my hardest to deal with my emotions in a way not to offend others, I finally just became numb to my own emotions. By the time I was a teenager, I had lost pretty much all trust in men. I didn't really have a father figure that I thought was worth looking up to. So, I turned to women.

A week before my 16th birthday, I officially started having feelings for a female. I simply did not want to deal with men. The girl that I was involved with was the best friend that I could have asked for. She was there to listen, she made time for me, and she never questioned anything that I told her. Her mother also played a big part in my journey. She was one of the easiest people in the world to talk to. I remember one night my mom and I started arguing about something and I got to the point where I didn't even want to look at her anymore. I didn't even bother putting on any shoes, before I walked all the way to the female's house in the dark. When I got there, I told her what was going on, and she just sat and listened to me. When her mother got home from work, I remember sitting down with her at their kitchen table and just pouring my heart out. I can still hear her say "Everything is going to be ok, baby." Then, she told me to get my stuff and she was taking me home because she was not going to come in between my mother and me.

When my friend's sister dropped me off back home, I had no idea what was in store for me. Does anybody remember the movie "Beloved"....when the old ladies were outside of the house praying for her to return to the dead? That's the scene that came to my head when I walked in the house. Nobody asked me if I was ok, nobody asked me if I wanted to talk. I walked into a living room of people just sitting there praying. Praying that the "lesbian demon" would flee from me.

Me being the person that I was at that age, didn't even allow it to bother me. I remember walking into my bedroom, closing my door, and waiting for everyone to leave.

At that point, I realized that I didn't have any one that I could really go to and just talk to. As parents that grew up in church, we sometimes think that calling everything a demon and praying will cause things to change. But we first have to find out what caused it. What I didn't realize was that I had never really learned what true love was, because I had never opened myself up to it. I confused the love of my friendship with a person for being in love with a person. Sadly enough, that just took me down a road that I wasn't ready to travel.

After finally breaking it off with her almost 2 years later, I wanted to leave everything that was familiar to me. I decided to move to Columbia, SC with some people that I had grown up with. I knew them all very well, and for the most part, we pretty much grew up in the same household for years. It was a two bedroom apartment, and I shared a room with one of the other girls. While there, I got my very first job at

Ashes No More

McDonalds. I was 17, living away from home, and I had a job- In my mind, I was GROWN!! I did not have a car, but one of my roommates worked there, as well, and when she didn't have to go in she just allowed me to drive her car. I actually enjoyed working there. I enjoyed talking to different people that did not know me at all, and sometimes being the only smiling face that some people saw during the day. My very first day there, I met one of the sweetest gentlemen that I have ever had the privilege to meet. I was new to the area, and pretty much had no friends, but he was there. He was the first male friend that I ever had….period. Over the time that I lived in Columbia, he not one time tried to do anything with me or push me past my limits. There was even one incident when my roommate had to work a double shift, and I didn't want to drive all the way home and then come right back and pick her up, so he asked if I wanted to come over to just spend some time with him while she worked. Mind you, it was about 3 in the morning, and I had only known him for about 3 months. Some people might look at this situation and say that was a dumb idea…but I beg to differ.

When we got to his house that he shared with his father, there was nobody else there. I still didn't feel uneasy. He never invited me into his bedroom, and he never even made a move. We sat in his living room for FOUR hours, just looking at pictures and telling stories about our lives.

Ashes No More

That was the night I realized that not *every* man was a bad man.

My time in Columbia was wonderful. I enjoyed every moment of it. I learned that not everyone was out to get me, and I met some people that will forever be in my heart. I even started going to church. The name of the church was Agape. It was something totally different, and it was just a sense of newness there. I had started to be a part of the Children's Church and both the Youth and Adult Choirs. I was attending Bible Studies when I wasn't working and I was attending functions there, not because someone was making me, but because I wanted to.

One night at choir rehearsal, the director called me over to him, and asked me to lead a song. At first, I said I didn't think that I was ready. I had just really started coming to church faithfully, and I didn't think that I was worthy of that duty. Some people might ask why. I will just say this. When I was in the world, I knew that I was wrong, and I didn't try to act as though I wasn't. I didn't sing in a choir, I didn't go to bible studies, I didn't go to revivals, and I didn't step foot in a church for a long time. Conviction was real to me, and I knew that I was not going to be what I had seen so many other people be in the church....a hypocrite.

But, I eventually said yes. When I did, he told me at that moment that things were about to change in my life, simply because of that "Yes". He told me that I had work to do in Columbia, and that it was meant for me to be there. The feeling that I felt in the pit of my stomach when he said those words to me were unexplainable. It was like a hot feeling in the pit of my stomach, mixed with butterflies, and a sensation of peace. That was the first time in a very long time that I had that feeling.

Not long after, some things started happening with the apartment that we were renting. We were giving our rent to one of the housemates that was in charge of handing in the rent. It turns out that they were not doing that with the money, and we ended up having to leave the apartment. Even in that, I didn't forget what the choir director told me, and I never even said that he was a "false prophet" or that he "didn't hear God". Being a part of that ministry, taught me a lot. One of the biggest things that I learned was that God has given us free will. Therefore, our actions can either bring God's word to pass or cause us to lose out. For example, If someone had told me that God said that I was going to get a job, and I never got up to look for one, or even got an offer and denied it...that doesn't mean that God didn't say it, that just means that I didn't do the work. And in this case, I could have fought to stay in Columbia. I am sure that some of the members would have allowed me to stay with them for a little while or even helped me to get a place. It was a choice that I made to give up on the fight, and leave. It was because of me that those things that were supposed to be completed by me went undone. Maybe, in a way, I just felt like it was too good to be true.

Being that I didn't feel like I had anyone else there, I ended up going back to live with my parents. But being back in that neighborhood brought back so many emotions and memories, that it was hard for me to focus on the big picture.

I started hanging around with the wrong people, and going places that I should not have been. I never tried drugs, and I never really liked the taste of alcohol, but I was just longing for attention and love in all the wrong places. The funny thing is that I never fit in, even when I tried to. I always knew that I wasn't doing the right things, and I knew that wasn't the life that I wanted to live, but I felt like I was too far gone by that point. I thought that I was simply too dirty for God to have to clean up.

Being that I was confused in so many ways, I set myself up for a lot of hurt.

Being back in town, I found myself in another harmful relationship. I was not attracted to females, and I knew it. The girl that I had been involved with before was just a great friend. She was just there for me when I needed someone the most. Her ears were constantly open to hear, and it seemed like her heart was always open to love. But, because I was confused, and felt like I was too far gone, I decided to get into a relationship with another female.

I was dating a girl that had a drug addiction, and I had no idea. When I look back at everything that happened, I wonder how I didn't know it. The truth is that I didn't see it because I wasn't looking for it, and I honestly had no idea what I should have been looking for.

When I moved back home, I was able to get another job, and I was able to get my first car. First of all, she didn't have a car and I did, so I drove everywhere. Because we lived in such a small town, people were always opening up little corner stores and selling things from their houses. So, there was a house in town that sold things like liquor and cigarettes. She would always ask me to take her there. She would buy gin…..and she would drink the entire thing every time. One day, she gave her money to someone to go get her something to drink, and when they snuck off with her $5.00 she went crazy! We searched for him for 6 hours….for $5.00. That was the first sign…..

Sign number two. One night, we were riding around, as usual, and she decided that she wanted to go to another little corner store in our town. When we got there, I saw some familiar faces from school, and I felt a little more comfortable. She asked me to take her and one of the guys there down the street. I did. When I got there, they got out of my car, and went into another car. It was around 10:30 at night by this time. I sat in my car and waited for her to come back to my car until 7:30 the next morning. I actually sat in a car alone in the woods waiting for someone to come back to MY car. I didn't realize then that I had sooo many angels watching over me. Anything could have happened to me. When I look back, I wonder what would have happened if they had decided to do whatever they were doing in my car. What if the cops had shown up? What if they had tried to get me to try it? What if I had gotten addicted?

It turns out that she was addicted to crack cocaine. I was never around anyone that did drugs like that, so I didn't know what signs to look out for. When she came back to the car (when the sun was already out) the first thing that she asked me was "Is there something in my nose?" I should have known then, but that was something that she was always asked, so I thought nothing of it. I also noticed that she had the jacket that she was wearing tied around her waist. Little did I know that she had gotten so high that she urinated on herself.

I know that a lot of people would have left someone like that after they found out the truth,

Ashes No More

but not someone that is looking for love. *I stayed*.

The final straw was soon to come though.

One night, we were looking for someplace to stay because her mother told her that she did not want her stepping foot in her house again and I KNEW that going to my house was out of the question. So, she had a cousin that had some vacant rental properties that we could spend a night in. I remember first meeting him and realizing that I had seen him a few times before. When I saw him he was out with his small children, playing in the park. This time when I saw him, he looked totally different. Nothing about him said "family man".

We followed him to the house, and he let us inside. When we got inside, I noticed that he had a few things there that most people wouldn't keep in a rental home. He had things like alcohol and a few chairs. It looked like it was a place that he went to when he wanted to get away from his family, or just get into trouble.

I told her that I was tired, and I wanted to go to sleep, so she made a pallet on the floor for me to lay down on. They stayed up and drank for a while, and she ended up falling asleep on my stomach. She was a very hard sleeper, and I always knew that, but this time I found out just how much of a bad thing that was.

I woke up in the middle of the night to someone whispering in my ear. I remember wanted to gag at the strong stench of alcohol. Her cousin waited for her to pass out, and then he made his move. I was laying on the floor, and she was knocked out on top of me. He knew that I could not move, so he took advantage of the situation. I remember hearing him tell me that he knew that I didn't want to be with her, and that he wanted to show me what I was missing out on. The exact words that I remember him using were "You're going to do what I say, and you're going to like it". That's the last thing that I heard before I started feeling his hands move up and down my legs. I remember laying there and crying silently. Some people might ask why I didn't scream. I didn't scream because I had given up on the power in my voice a long time ago. I didn't think that screaming would do anything to help the situation. So, I just laid there with my eyes closed and tears running down my face with a drunk person laying on top of me, and a pervert doing what he wanted.

The next morning, I lost my job because I didn't show up. I was just so upset with myself and my life. I didn't even want to go home. I seriously just wanted to find a box, and curl up under a bridge some place. At least, then things would be expected to go wrong. It wouldnt seem like such a shock when things would happen, and things wouldn't hurt, as much.

Ashes No More

At that point in my life, I had pretty much had
enough of people in general. I didn't even
understand why I was going through so much at
the time. I wasn't even 20 years old yet, and I
felt like I had experienced so much more than I
needed to. But I had no idea that these things
were all sprouting from the seed that was
planted in me when I was 7 years old. But once
again, even through all of that, God had his
angels encamped all around me. I never knew
what type of love I was supposed to be looking
for, so I didn't know what kind of love was wrong.
I knew a lot of things were wrong, but I didn't
feel like anyone had taken the time to teach me
how to do things right. I was only 18, but I had
escaped death more times than I could have
counted. I didn't realize how many times I could
have been killed and left for dead until I got
older and looked back.

The girl that was addicted to drugs actually
started stalking me when I stopped talking to her.
I didn't even know that she was parking next to
my house, by my room window, watching me
until one of my neighbors told me. And when I
called to confront her about it, she told me that
she was not going to stop. I literally had to call
the cops and get a restraining order against her.
This was a girl that I had seen pull out a knife on
her own sister in the middle of a fight. I don't
know what made me think that she wouldn't

have done the same thing to me if we got into an argument.

My life had taken a dive into the worst direction. I was not sure what my next steps were going to be, but I was definitely sure that I did not want to live the rest of my life the way that it was starting to go. I had gotten used to abuse. I was numb to it. I didn't even look at it the same way anymore. It simply became a part of life. The saddest thing was that I believed that in my heart. I knew that God was a God of love, but I didn't feel like I was worth being loved my Him. I felt like I deserved the struggle and like I deserved the abuse.

I am a firm believer that for every action, there is a reaction. There is a reason for everything that we do, and every feeling that we feel. When I was first sexually abused, I was left with someone because I didn't listen to my mother when she told me to get ready to go. I felt like I was being punished because I didn't listen. That stigma and that feeling stuck with me for all of those years, and I didn't even realize that I was still carrying it. I felt like I still deserved to be punished, so I didn't fight it.

> *Romans 15:5*
>
> *Now may the God who gives the power of patient endurance and Who supplies encouragement, grant you to live in such mutual harmony and such full*

sympathy with one another, in accord with Christ Jesus.

Newness in the Making

Good Morning

Psalm 139:13-14

For thou hast possessed my reins; thou hast covered me in my mother's womb. I will praise thee; for I am fearfully and wonderfully made; marvelous are thy works; and that my soul knoweth right well.

At the ripe age of 19 years old, I finally made up in my mind to do the right thing, and live the way that I knew I should have been living all along. That was not as easy of a decision to

Ashes No More

make as most people would think. After all that happened to me growing up, most people would have been jumping to the altar. I was not that person. I really did believe that I didn't deserve that chance. I have a story behind that, too, of course.

I finally began dating a gentleman that I met at a job that I started. He was a very nice guy, and he treated me with the upmost respect. I thought that I was doing pretty well for myself. I was even thinking about attempting to go to church.

In the meantime, I was still friends with some people that I knew I should not have been friends with. I was hanging out with them all times of night, and this time I knew for a fact that they were doing things that they should not have been doing. I knew that most of them were using me for a ride and the fact that they knew that I was not going to tell them no. They also knew that I was still known as a good girl, and that nobody was suspect anything if they saw me. And because I knew that I wasn't ever really going to fit in, I just became complacent in the fact that people were going to treat me that way.

I had been over to a friend's house all day long, and I decided to go home to take a shower and a quick nap. Of course, when I was over there, I always felt funny, but feeling funny was better than feeling unwanted. When I woke up, I got dressed, and started looking for my keys to go out of the door. I remember getting so frustrated that I could not find my car keys. I literally was about to have a fit. I remember arguing with my mom because I was mad that I couldn't find my keys. Finally, I just went to my room, and went back to sleep because I knew that arguing was going to get me nowhere.

The crazy thing about this time is that when I woke up the next morning, I found my keys with no problem. But before I could even walk out of the house, I found out that the house that I was trying to go to burned down the night before. They said that because it was an old house, there were some electrical problems, and that's what cause a fire to break out in the middle of the night. I was so distraught, because I knew that I could have been there, and I knew that I could have been the one that got left in the fire. I could have been the one that died, because I wanted to feel wanted. I am not sure to this day if my mother hid my keys because she knew something was going to happen, or if the angels simply saved my life....either way...I was appreciative to still be alive.

BUT, that still didn't make me totally surrender to God. I did start going to church though... and I started seeing a gentleman there. He was a musician, and he lived a few towns over. My neighbor at the time was a pastor that had moved to SC a few years prior. I would see them going and coming to church all the time, and my mother was very close with them. They had invited me to go to church with them a few times, and avoiding them seemed to be the easiest answer. One day, I finally said yes, and that's when things started to change for the better. It was a start.

The gentleman that I was involved in was definitely different. I really don't quite remember how we even started talking, but I do know that my former pastor had something to do with it. I think that he was just happy to see that I was dating a guy, and that the guy was in church. What caught me by surprise was his past. I knew that I had had a past, and that I was not ever expecting to be with someone that had done nothing, but this guy had major anger issues. He had even gone to court for wrapping the gas line around someone's neck at a gas station and threatening to light a match. He had no idea how to handle his emotions, and that was something I didn't trust. When we would have disagreements, he would yell in my face, or threaten to put his hands on me. Abuse just seemed to be something that I couldn't get away from.

My mother and I actually talked about our relationship, one day. I can remember sitting on the floor in our living room, while she did my hair. She asked me how I felt about him, and I told her that I liked him, but I didn't want to be

Ashes No More

married to him. Everyone seemed to be wanting me to marry him, and I just knew better. My mother and I actually got a lot closer, as I got older, and she became one of the easiest people for me to talk to about relationships. And every time, she told me that it was my decision.

But, while him and I were dating, people just always tried to push us into marriage. One night, we were riding home from church, and he was saying that he was tired. He brought up the fact that he might stay at the hotel in our town until the next morning, and then drive home. My pastor was in the front seat, and I was in the back seat. When the guy suggested that, my pastor looked at me and asked me if I was going to stay with him. I was in so much shock, that I couldn't even respond right away. I may not have been living right, but I knew what the bible said. My response was "We aren't married.".....and my pastor's response was "But y'all will be".

I didn't quite look at him the same after that, but I knew that this was probably the only opportunity that I had to be in some type of atmosphere of worship, and I needed it.

At the time, I was not technically a "member", but I was more faithful to that ministry than I had been to anything in my life.

During this time, I learned the basic fundamentals of ministry. I learned about prayer, fasting, warfare, witchcraft, speaking in tongues, and the meaning of true worship. I had been in church all of my life, and I had been taught many things, but had yet to experience lots of things for myself. Being a part of this ministry gave me the opportunity to put all the lessons that I had been taught to use....and it was definitely an experience.

The two things that I learned that stuck with me the most were WORSHIP and WARFARE. I will get into worship a little later, but let me explain my most vivid experience with warfare. There was a gentleman preacher that had been fellowshipping with my former pastor for a while. I had not met him yet, but I had heard lots of stories about him from them. My mother even went to go meet him before I did. When she went though, she had a totally different take on him and the spirit that he had. I remember them teasing my mother for soo long because they said she was being dramatic. The night that she met him she cried the entire ride home, because she said that it was just something about him that she didn't like, but that she couldn't put her finger on it.

When I met him, I really didn't know what to expect. At the time, my discernment was nowhere nearly as keen as it is now. All I knew was that there was this man that was preaching what seemed to be everywhere, and people always seemed to flock to him.

I remember the first time that I knew that something was wrong with the situation. We went along with my former pastor to a service that this Prophet was having. When we got there, the sanctuary was very dark. I don't remember seeing but 3 men in the service. One was my former pastor, the other was the hosting Prophet, and the third was his armor bearer. I felt a little uncomfortable, so I just did what I always did, and watched. As time went on, I remember hearing him say these words...."Go get my chair". From that statement, his armor bearer went into what I am assuming was his office, and brought back this huge chair and sat it where the altar was. The chair looked like it was for a King. He sat in the chair, and pulled out a bottle of what looked like extra virgin olive oil (which is normally used during most prayer services). When he began to put it on people, an odor began to fill the room. It was an odor that I wasn't expecting to smell at that time. What it turned out to be was garlic oil (which was supposedly used to ward off evil spirits).

If that wasn't bad enough, I then remember him calling all the Pastors to the altar, and handing them some fruit. He then told them to eat the "Fruit of the Spirit". I still remember the look of confusion and frustration on my former pastor's face. He looked so disgusted and ready to walk out. He took the fruit, and when he wasn't looking he put it in his pocket and later threw it into the lake right next to the church.

That still was not the end of the service. He later started playing some type of music and singing some song that he made up. He then walked around the congregation, of women, and began to kiss some of the women….saying that God told him to "Greet them with a holy kiss".

That was the moment I think I became more confused. I knew what was going on the world, and all of the perversion that I had encountered and known about. I knew that there were people out there that simply lived to prey on people that they felt were "easy targets". What I did NOT know was that was something was going on in the church……openly.

Ill never forget being in New York for one of his services. We got out of church kid of late, and we went to a restaurant not too far away afterwards. He must have had some "pull", because the restaurant that we went to was actually closed, but they opened it up just for him. It was about 20 of us sitting at the table, and his wife had gone home for some reason. He has a small son that was with him though. He asked his son a question that I had never heard anyone ask their child. The question was "Where do you want your next sister or brother to come from? The North, South, East, or West?"

I kept a very close eye on him from that moment on. I accompanied my former pastor and his family to New York where he had to speak for this same man, and I will just say that everything was an "experience". He then set up camp at another church in our town, and began to have services there on a regular basis. He had a room there that he set up as his office. He had a broom hanging on the wall in the office. It was one of those brooms that a lot of older people hung up on their walls for decoration. Every time that someone came into the office to speak to him, he would take it down and put it over your head...he would call it "sweeping out your mind". He also had pictures of himself that he would actually sell after his services for people to hang on their walls so that he could "watch over their home".

The experience that I remember the most from when he was ministering in our town was when I went to go meet with him one night. I was 19 years old, and he had come to me about becoming his administrative assistant and traveling with him. Of course, my mother had already let me know that was not the will of the Lord, but that I still needed to pray about it. I did not just want to flat out say "no". So, I decided that I would just go talk to him and let him know that I wasn't going to be able to do that because I was about to start school, and had a plethora of other opportunities coming my way.

Ashes No More

When I walked in there, the office was very dark. As soon as I stepped foot in there, he took the broom and shook it over my head. He then came over to give me a hug. When he hugged me, he started off with his hands on my back, and then quickly moved his hands down to my butt. He squeezed it firmly, and wouldn't let me go. I remember my body freezing at that moment, and my eyes welling up with water. I remember asking God at that moment if this is what I was put on earth to endure.

When I finally pulled myself away, he just looked at me with a smile on his face and said "What's wrong? Are you okay?" It caught me off guard because I felt like he was mocking me. He smirked and started an entire conversation as if nothing had happened.

I was never quite the same after that. I went to church, and I did the things that I was supposed to do….but with no trust in my heart. That's when worship came into play.

I had actually fallen in love with worship before I even knew what it really was. I just knew that certain songs and certain times took me to a place that I didn't want to leave. Shouting and dancing was wonderful. It served its purpose, and then some. But it didn't do it for me like worship. I found myself listening to the same songs at night before I went to sleep, because I wanted to sleep in that mode. I read my bible daily, and I even went weeks without television. I just wanted to be in His presence. I wanted to feel His love.

One night, my mother and I were on our way to church, and I prayed the whole way there. When we got there, there was a minister already up praying. Even though she was talking to us, it seems like she was talking at us. I just continued to pray. All of a sudden, my former pastor stopped her right in the middle of her prayer, told her that she could have a seat, and told me to come up and pray. I could not believe that he had actually called me up there to pray. I didn't really think that I was worthy of doing it in public, because of all the things that I had done in the world. The lady that was up before he called me had been in ministry for decades, so I didn't understand why he would call me.

I decided to be obedient, and I stepped up to the plate. I closed my eyes, and began to pray the same exact way that I prayed when I was alone in my room. I began to cry out to God and just embrace His presence. When I finally opened my eyes, I could tell that something was different. It was as if the room had gotten lighter. Not because I prayed, but because I allowed Him to take control of the atmosphere with no interference from me or my emotions.

Proverbs 19:20-21

Ashes No More

*Hear counsel and receive instruction,
that thou mayest be wise in thy latter
end. There are many devices in a
man's heart; nevertheless the counsel
of the Lord, that shall stand.*

A New Experience

The Same Hurt

2 Thessalonians 3:3

But the Lord is faithful, who shall stablish you, and keep you from evil.

I finally decided that I wanted to go back to school. I had talked about it a few times before, and I actually had gotten into quite a few colleges, but all of the ones that I really wanted to attend were out of state, and my mother convinced me that that was not going to work out.

I was still in the church, and I will living at "holy" as I could live, but of course that still

Ashes No More

wasn't good enough. I remember my mom pulling me aside and telling me that she was going to take me to a clinic. The purpose was for birth control. I really didn't understand why, because I had not too long ago started talking to men, so that was definitely out of the question, as far as I was concerned. But it turned out that she was taking me because a pastor had mentioned to someone else that they didn't think that I was going to make it out of college without having a baby, and she didn't want that to come to pass.

I was actually supposed to go to South Carolina State University. I even went to the campus to get my dorm and everything, and when I got there, they were so unorganized that we just decided to go next door. At this time in my life, my mother had started to private duty nursing. She just so happened to be taking care of the mother of someone that had a lot of "pull" at Claflin University. He got me in there and in a dorm the same day.

After getting settled in I thanked God for such a wonderful opportunity. I told myself that I was going to just start over and forget about the past. I was going to create some new positive memories, and make my own path worth the journey. I was content and at peace at that moment.

It just so happened that a lot of people from my high school had gone off to go to Claflin

University. So, I felt more at home being there around people that I had gone to high school with.

I hung out with five main females. Two of them happened to go to my high school. There were three more girls that were around, but one of them ended up leaving and I wasn't all that close to the other. So, it was mostly me and the three main females most of the time. None of us had cars, so we usually walked anyplace that we wanted to go. Thursday night was always "College Night" at all of the clubs, and we usually made it there before 10, so that we could get in for free. I had never been in a club before, but I guess I fit right in. Dancing was always something that I loved to do, and to me, that was the whole purpose of going. I wasn't naïve enough to believe that I was going to find my husband in the club, but I did enjoy going there for the fun of it and meeting new people.

Most of the guys there were from South Carolina State. Not too many guys from Claflin University were going to be found out during the week like that. Claflin was a very strict school that had curfews and consequences for not following the rules.

One night, we decided to go to a party at a club. When we got there, it was crowded, as usual. It seemed to be extra hot. We never drank when we went out, but I remember the smell of alcohol and smoke being almost overwhelming in the building. It seemed like everyone was there from almost every college in the area. All of a sudden, everyone ran to one side of the building. Me being the person that I am, I ran along with them, but I had no idea what I was running to or from. When I asked my friend why we were running, her response was, "Girl, you ain see that boy with a gun in the middle of the floor????" To this day, I don't remember seeing him, even after she tried to point him out to me. But I didn't need to see him to believe that he had a gun. Just then, the cops threw in what they called some "smoke bombs", causing everyone to run outside of the building. When we got outside, we were literal ducking down and trying to make sure that the coast was clear. I just kept hearing gun shots back and forth. People went to their cars and got guns to go back and forth with each other. I remember thinking that I could die that night. I could be the one to get shot out of all the people there, simply because I knew that I didn't belong there in the first place.

We rode back to the dorm with a friend, and the entire time, I kept thinking that *God had protected me once again*.

There were so many times when I was in college that the Lord saved me from harm. I am forever grateful for all that He has done for me. All the times when I could have gone home with people that I did not know, and ended up in somebody's ditch. All the times when I know that I could have contracted diseases or ended up pregnant. God not only protected my body, but he protected my mind.....in the midst of everything that happened to me. Again I say, in the midst of *everything* that happened to me.

One night, I went out with my friends, and I met this guy. I had seen him a couple of times before, but I never knew his name or anything about him. He was always with another guy that I had encountered a few times that was a part of a well-known fraternity on campus. The guy that I had encountered was always very nice, and always had a smile on his face. He always complimented me, but not in an uncomfortable way. He would always ask me to dance, and he never tried anything with me. This night in particular, he decided to introduce me to his friend. His friend was handsome, but he was very quiet. As, I stated before, I had seen him around but I never spoke to him.

His friend started a conversation with me, and he seemed to be very interesting. We talked the entire night while we were out, and then he asked for my number. Before I could get back to my dorm, he had already texted me. When I got back to the dorm, he decided to call me. I didn't have a roommate, so he and I literally talked on the phone until the sun came up. Once the sun came up, he asked me if I wanted to go to breakfast down the street. I agreed, and asked for some time to freshen up. He came about an hour later, and when he came and got me, we went to breakfast at the IHOP down the street. I remember looking into his eyes, and thinking that there was something about him that seemed so familiar, but I couldn't think of what it was. So, I just let it go, and continued to enjoy his conversation.

When we got back in the car, he proceeded to go in the opposite direction of the school. I asked him where we were going, and he said that he had to go back to his house for something. I felt *very* uncomfortable when he said that, but I tried to play it off with a joke about not knowing him well enough to go to his home (even though I was serious).

The rest of the ride seemed like the longest ride in the world. It seemed like we were driving so slowly that I could count the trees. I could hear every bird chirp and every bug buzz. There seemed to be no more wonderful conversation between the two of us. I had moved over closer to the door, and every time that he stopped at a light, I wanted to jump out of the truck and run somewhere......anywhere.

My eyes began to swell with water, but I took a few deep breathes because I didn't want him to think anything. I had learned throughout my experiences in life that I if a man wanted to do something, he was going to do it. And the more you fought, the harder it was going to be for **you**!

What seemed liked centuries passed, and we finally got to his house. I felt a little better when he told me that he lived with his parents. I began to think that maybe I was overthinking the situation. Maybe every guy wasn't out to try to take advantage of me. Maybe this time, he really did like me and wanted to be a friend first. I didn't see "his parents" car in the driveway, but I thought that maybe it was in the garage. I didn't want to ask, because I didn't want to seem suspicious, but I asked anyway. His response was that they were supposed to be home by now, and that they should be home soon.

I could have jumped out of my skin at that very moment......

When we got in the house, it seemed to be just as empty as the way my heart was. I could have whispered and heard an echo from it. I don't remember seeing any pictures on the walls, or anything that said "family". I asked him if this was the house that he had grown up in, and he told me that it was. When I asked about pictures or paintings on the wall, I could see the frustration and aggravation building up in him.

Ashes No More

Once he calmed down, we began to talk. I don't remember exactly what we were talking about, but I do remember the fact that he was very short. He had been talking almost nonstop for 12 hours, but at this moment, he didn't have much to say. So, of course, I began to get short with my words because it's simply no fun talking to yourself.

He offered me something to drink, and I didn't feel comfortable, so I said no. At that moment, I saw his face go blank, as if I had called him out of his name or something. I tried my hardest not to allow the fear that I had inside of me at that very moment to seep out. It was like he wanted me to take the drink for a specific reason. I'd learned that you don't take drinks from just anybody, because people could put things in them. Especially if you didn't see them make the drink. But I had no idea that that was the least of my worries….what happened next was like something out of a movie.

All of a sudden, someone came up behind me and covered my mouth and nose. Before I could even think, my eyes and nose were burning, and then everything went blank. They drugged me with some type of liquid on a cloth, and caused me to pass out.

When I woke up, thing were a little blurry. I had a headache that couldn't be explained, and my nose burned like crazy. But what shocked me the most was that the guy was standing over me. Not only was he there, but the friend that introduced us was there. He was the one that came up behind me when I didn't take the drink that was offered. I just remember tears running down my eyes. My pants were off and my panties were down to my ankles. My shirt had been ripped, and my bra had been lifted up. I could smell the stench of the guy's cologne. I didn't scream because I didn't see the point in screaming. I didn't think that it would have helped in any way. *I had again lost all power in my voice.*

They didn't bother tying me up or anything because the drug was so strong that I didn't feel anything. So, when they saw me moving around, they looked scared. I remember them running out of the room and I could hear them mumbling to each other. Trying to come up with a plan, I guess. When they came back in the room, I just said in a faint voice "If you let me go, I won't tell." I don't think they believed me, but I don't think that they expected me to wake up when I did either. The guy that introduced the other guy to me came over to me with a huge knife in his hands, and assured me that if I ever told anyone, then he would make sure that the next time he got me alone; he would finish it the way he *planned.*

They pretty much dragged me to the car and threw me in the back seat. The entire ride back to campus, I just prayed and cried. The prayer that I prayed in the car was not a prayer to ask for anything or a prayer for him to do anything. It was simply *"God, because of this-I KNOW you're real."* At that moment, riding in the back of that car I realized that I could have died...again. I prayed a prayer of affirmation because that affirmed to me that He was real. He had saved my life...again.

They didn't even drive me back on campus. They dropped me off around the corner, and made me walk back to campus. I had no idea what time it was, and my phone had died. The college that I attended was a very structured campus, so after around 8 pm....you weren't going to see too many people outside. I figured it was around that time, because I saw no one. Walking back to my dorm, I remember feeling all alone. I felt like I had no one. Even though I knew that God was real, I didn't know why I had to go through all the things that I had endured so far in life. I knew that there had to be a reason, but I didn't understand why I had to be that example.

After managing to get all the way to my dorm building, without seeing one person, I went into my room and locked the door. I know longer had a roommate, and was happy about that at first. But at that moment, I would have done anything to have someone in that room when I stepped foot in there. The reality was what it was though. There was nobody there but me. I didn't even make it to my bed. I just walked in the door and fell to the floor. I balled up like a baby, and I just cried. I cried into the hands of God. I cried from the depths of my soul. I cried like the little girl that I felt that I was, deep inside.

When I finally got up, I just wanted to clean myself. I had been drugged and raped was my assumption. I didn't even know what they did to me. The only reason that I knew that they had done something was because other than the fact that my clothes were messed up when I finally woke up, I knew my body, and I didn't feel right. I just kept thinking about all the things that they could have done to me. The smell of their cologne seemed to be on every inch of me. When I took a shower, I stayed in there for over an hour-just scrubbing. I wanted the dirt and the filth to just go away. I wanted to wash away the memories of every person that had every violated me. I wanted to scrub away the hurt that I felt and the distrust that I had grown for both men and women.

It was at that moment that I realized that I hated sex. My deepest scars in life had come from sexual perversion, and I wanted nothing to do with it. I hated sex.

My Pieces

These are my pieces, but not my whole.
I am more than this flesh and blood.
My skin does not portray who/what lies beneath.

Ashes No More

*My smile does not really show how I feel
and my eyes do not allow you to see my depth.*

*I am no longer an object of someone else's will,
but a prisoner to my own body.
My body does not feel like it belongs to me.
For so long it was not given a say
and was forcibly maneuvered by another.*

*Even my mind seems to be dictated
by my own body's sensations.
A simple touch of my arm can trigger a memory.
My hand hesitates to make contact
with even ones I love.*

*All of these pieces while built together,
feel disjointed.
My lips long for a compassionate kiss,
but my hand will freely push it away.
My arms cry out to be wrapped in another's,
but my body quickly tightens
responding to a perceived attack.
My body, hidden
is self-conscious
of how it will be judged.
It is a vessel of unknown.*

*Each touch is a switch
that triggers a new or old memory.
A personal home theater of years past,
many showing reruns that had long been
forgotten
or simply waiting for the right time.
My home movies are nightmares*

Ashes No More

that give understanding to my body's reactions.
Unlike nightmares, I cannot wake up
and say it was just a dream.

I have tried to rationalize
with both my mind and body, but it yields to the
past.
They are a great puzzle
that I am slowly piecing together.
The picture of who I am
becomes clearer with each piece,
and like most children's toys, the result is often
not as spectacular as you had hoped.

Can I see who I am becoming
without finishing the puzzle?
The pieces have slowly come together
to create a gruesome picture of who I was.
The pieces cannot be reconfigured
to change the ultimate image;
my picture of my past will always be the same

By my vision of the future, is in my hands.

Proverbs 3:11-12

My son, despise not the chastening of
the Lord; neither be weary of his
correction. For whom the Lord loveth

Ashes No More

he correcteth; even as a father, the son in whom he delighteth.

Not Quite a Lady

Turning the Page

Psalm 55:22

Cast thy burden upon the Lord, and He shall sustain thee; He shall never suffer the righteous to be moved.

For a long time after that incident, I didn't look at people the same. To this day, I still deal with some issues because of that experience in particular. After finally coming to terms with the fact that I could have contracted anything from that, and taking myself to a clinic to make sure that I didn't- I still felt like I caught something. Even though I was "clean", and the results of every test came back negative....I still felt like I was somehow sick. That's when I realized that most diseases kill you slowly, while you are yet getting treatment; but some scars are so deep that you don't even know that you need treatment, and therefore slowly begin to ALLOW yourself to die.

Ashes No More

I knew that I needed help. But I had no idea where to turn to. Men had used me. Women had used me. Even Pastors and Elders in the church had used me. There was no one person in my life that I could go to about the situation. I wasn't a very outgoing person, because of all the things that had happened-and after the last experience, I definitely wasn't about to start. All I wanted was a place to belong. I desired to be loved for the right reasons, and cared about sincerely.

Every time that I would look back at all the things that happened, and all the times that I could have died, and felt like without a doubt I should have died- I just didn't see why I didn't. Again, I knew that God had a plan for my life, but I didn't see why I was even still an option to be used. I felt like I was so unworthy at this point, that He needed to just pass over me and go to the next person. Better yet, He could have just moved me out of the way.

Sometimes because of things that we go through, we feel like God simply has better options. It still baffles me that He can love us unconditionally. We use that term so loosely in life and in ministry, but it is such a strong word. *Unconditionally* means no matter what. After all the times that I had been touched inappropriately, and all the times that I had messed up on my own, He still loved me the same.

Ashes No More

After many restraining orders and threats against the guys that abused me that night, I made the decision that I was not going to go back to that school the next term. The fact that the school had somehow magically lost all record of my grades and attendance for the whole semester just made the decision a lot easier. So, then my concern became "What do I do with my life now?" At this point, I was just filled with a lot of fear and disappointment. I was afraid to go to church, afraid of relationships, afraid to even live on a college campus, and afraid to be loved.

I had never known the real meaning of love. People say this all the time, but I really had no clue. All the people that were put in my life to love me had disappointed me, left me, or hurt me; and all of the people that I chose to put in my life had done the same. Love was something that I would not have been able to handle, even if it came to me at that point. But at this point, I would have just taken a hug. I really longed for was a hug.....*just a hug*.

For a while, I just stayed to myself. I avoided the church and people from church. The summer after I left school, I spent most of my time just reflecting on all that had happened to me and wondering what the next step was going to be. I felt like I was not clean enough to be in the presence of God, and that I was too tainted to be loved by anybody else. I knew that I HAD a calling on my life, but I thought that I had

Ashes No More

strayed too far away to actually get back on track. There were so many nights that I cried myself to sleep, and felt like I was never going to make it in this world. I actually got to the point where I told myself that hell was my home, and that this world was just preparing me for it.

This is where I learned the severity of depression. It is something that people take so lightly, but that weighs on you very heavily. Now, I can say that I wasn't in the state of depression for an extended period of time, because for a while, I was just caught up in my emotions and didn't know how to move on from the past. There is seriously a difference. Once I got into a state of depression, I didn't care about my emotions or my past….I simply didn't want to "be" anymore. I just wanted to curl up in a dark room and stay there until the end of time. I didn't want to face the world or anything that came along with it. The place of depression only lasted about two weeks, before I had a dream………

Psalm 8:4

Ashes No More

What is man that You are mindful of him, and the son of man that You care for him?

The Power of Dreams....

Taking a Step

Psalm 33:4

For the word of the Lord is right; and all His work is done in faithfulness.

When in depression, sleep is usually a huge part of your day and night. So, on this particular night, I didn't have any reason to think that it would be any different. I went to sleep at around 6:30 pm, after just lying there and waiting for the sun to go down. I don't remember much about what was going through my mind, but what I do remember is the dream that I had, once I had finally drifted off.

Ashes No More

I am not a deep or complex person, and it really doesn't take a lot to get a message through to me. So, this was not a long dream. All I remember is darkness. Have you ever been in a place that was so dark that you kept blinking repeatedly and stretching your eyelids, hoping that maybe you would be able to see something?? Well, that's where I was. There was nothing but darkness around me. I had no idea what I was standing on or even what was around me. All of a sudden, whatever it was that I was standing on....vanished, and I just began to fall. The speed at which I felt that I was falling was unreal. I remember keeping my mouth and eyes closed, while tears fell from my face. Then, I heard a voice say two simple words. Those words were, "Look up". The moment I looked up, things changed. I had a floor to stand on (a foundation), the lights came on, and I was in a room with what seemed like a million doors. That's when I realized that the solution to all that I was going through was very simple. All I had to do was look up, and things would change for the better.

And even though I knew that was what I needed to do, I still didn't quite know how I would get to that point. All I could do was take it one day at a time.

I started going to church and talking to God more than ever. I know that people always say that you cant change over night, but I literally did in sooo many ways. I went and had my phone

Ashes No More

number changed, I didn't reach out to anyone that was negative in my life, I had a goal in mind...and I was going to do all that I needed to do to reach that goal.

It took some time for me to get to the place where I was comfortable enough to open up to people, but it happened after some time.

After some time of being on the right track again, my former pastor received an engagement in Charlotte, NC. Now what is crazy is that the young man who was hosting the service had come in contact with me about a year ago at a month long tent revival in a small town close to where I lived. I still remembered exactly what he had on and even the word that was given to him that night through my pastor. Mind you, I had no idea that our paths would cross again, but when they did, I knew that it was not a coincidence.

So, the week of the engagement, I fasted and prayed. In the beginning, my mother and I were not going to be able to go, but at the last minute things changed. I had no idea as to why I was so nervous, but I would soon find out.

When we finally got there, the service was amazing. The worship was unbelievable, and hospitality was great. The young man that was hosting the conference did a wonderful job. The first night, after service, he led us to the store to pick up a couple of things because we didn't know our way around. The second night though, we ended up going to get a late dinner after service. Him and I didn't really talk a whole lot at the restaurant, but when he led us to the hotel, he stayed around for a while. We actually stayed up and talked until 6 o'clock the next morning, without losing conversation. It's like we were able to get to know each other in one night.

One thing about me is that I always told the truth about my past and the things that I went through. Some people say that is a not a good thing and you shouldn't always tell people everything, but I learned that when you are transparent, there aren't any surprises later on. You don't have to worry about anyone questioning you or feeling like you "withheld the truth".

That was a night that I will never forget. I felt like everything that I had gone through in relationships had just prepared me for that moment.

The next day, it was time to leave. We exchanged numbers, and I can honestly say that we haven't gone a day without talking since then. Things did move very fast with us though. Within about two weeks, we were officially dating. He would drive down to South Carolina on the weekends, being that he also had family there, as well. That lasted for about two months, before his mother called my phone because of a "situation", looking for him. Some things had

Ashes No More

happened, and she didn't have anyone to babysit his little sister, while she worked in the afternoons. I do remember that it was the weekend of my 20th birthday, when I made the decision to pack up and move to Charlotte to help out his family. After only dating for two months.

Within those months that we dated, we endured and supported each other through more things that most people don't have to go through for the first few years of an actual marriage.

Even though things seemed to be tense at times when it came to the people around us and their circumstances, everyone seemed to be ok with our relationship. And because we were both young and wanted to do things the right way, we prayed and asked God what our purpose was for the connection between the two of us. Once we had both heard from God concerning our relationship, we decided to take it to the next level and talk about marriage.

After exactly six months and one day of dating, we said our vows before God and one witness in a park in Moncks Corner, SC at 6:30 pm. That was one of the absolute greatest moments in my life. I couldn't have asked for anything more. Even though we did not have a huge wedding or anything spectacular, the intimacy that we shared was something that I couldn't have ever imagined.

Ashes No More

For an entire year, we didn't tell anyone that we were married. He lived in Charlotte, while I lived in South Carolina. We traveled back and forth every weekend for a few months, because we were both in college. It was definitely a testament to our commitment, early on in our relationship.

Isaiah 32:17

And the effect of righteousness will be peace, and the result of righteousness will be quietness and confident trust forever.

A Fresh Start

Two become one...........

Ezekial 36:26

A new heart will I give you and a new spirit will I put within you, and I will take away the stony heart from your flesh and give you a heart flesh.

During those times of us being together, and not living in the same area, a lot of things happened. My husband found out some things about his life that he never knew about, in the midst of dealing with some issues from experiences from his upbringing. Meanwhile, I was still dealing with a lot of issues from my childhood, and the experiences that I had growing up.

We had no choice but to be each the support system that each other needed to get over some things. There were many nights that we cried and had no idea what we were going to do. From day one, it was him and I against the world. We really didn't have anyone else that we could go to when we needed someone to talk to in the beginning of our marriage. And we didn't really have any marriages close to us that we could look up to or have as an example. We had to learn from and teach each other.

So, in the midst of everything...my husband let me know that it was time for him to launch back into ministry. He had already been ordained as a Pastor by someone else that had practically left him with no instruction. Because of that, he sat down for about a year, so that he could hear from God and do things the way that He would want him to.

When he said that it was time, we moved immediately and found a building. With neither of us working and both of us in school, it was very hard to keep going back and forth. I ended up just moving to Charlotte, and my husband and I actually lived in the church for almost 6 months. And when I say that we lived in the church, I mean those exact words... we *lived* in the church. We had a refrigerator in the kitchen area, and we always did a lot of cooking for services, so we always had leftovers for us to eat on. One of the church mothers gave us a hot plate, and we cooked MANY meals on that! Our main meals were hamburger helper, ramon noodles, and spaghetti. We slept on an air mattress in the office, and sometimes we would move it into the foyer, when it got too hot in there. I cried so

Ashes No More

many tears in those six months. I couldn't understand why we had to go through that.

I just didn't understand how people were out there that weren't doing right and treating people badly, but still sleeping in a warm bed at night…while my husband and I were sleeping on the floor in a warehouse building. But I will say one thing, we prayed more than ever! We were at the altar ALL the time.

Eventually, we went to stay with my husband's mom. That only lasted about a month, because we just felt like we were taking on responsibilities that didn't belong to us. By this time, though, my husband had gotten a job at a local grocery store, and I was enrolled in school again. So, one of our ministers allowed us to stay with her until we found a place of our own.

That's when all craziness first broke lose. I still remember the day HE got the phone call. It was one of his family members on the phone, and she had some news for him. No one had died, and no accident had happened. There was no sickness to talk about, and there was nothing urgent to discuss…….so I thought.

The phone call was to tell him that I had a past. Two of his family members had literally gotten together to have a "meeting" about me dating females in my past. They told him that I was a "dyke" and that I was known around town. Now, one thing about me is that I never slept around.

Ashes No More

If I was doing something, I didn't hide it very much. And if you asked me, I definitely told the truth. So, when they started talking, I already knew that some things were going to be exaggerated. But what they didn't know was that I had told him everything from day one. He didn't have to ask me...I volunteered to tell him. What I didn't know, was that this was the beginning of a world of secrets.

I had never been in that place before. I thought that him and I were going to just fall in love, move on from our pasts, and just live happily ever after. Even with all that had happened in my past, I had never been in a place where I had to love someone and have issues with their family. I had wonderful relationships with the families of everyone that I had ever been with, up until this point. And from what I thought, I had a wonderful relationship with them, until James and I mentioned getting married. Up until then, everyone seemed to love me and think that I was a wonderful person. They never questioned anything that we did. But it just seemed like the minute that we mentioned making it permanent, it became the talk of the family.

I think what hurt me the most, was the fact that no one ever once came to me to talk to me about it. Even after James told them that it hurt me and that they were causing confusion, they simply apologized to *him* and to this day, has never said anything to me about the situation.

Ashes No More

BUT even after all of that, he still chose to make me his wife.

And after almost a year of being married, we decided to have a ceremony….for the people. That in itself was another test for us. We really only had one so that people wouldn't be wondering if him and I were just "shacking up". We just wanted it to be out in the open. The sad thing was that only a few of my husband's family members showed up. We later found out that one family member told the others that we didn't want anyone there, and they believed that person instead of just coming and asking us. We had out ceremony in South Carolina, but we didn't even stay overnight. We drove straight back to Charlotte after the ceremony.

It was only by the favor of God that we found an apartment only a few weeks after moving in with the minister. So, when we went back home, we had our own place to go to. Not only did we find a place, but the blessings that came along with the place showed that God was putting his "seal of approval" on our union. We were SOMEHOW approved for a two bedroom, two bathroom apartment with NO deposit. Not only that, but they had a special going where if you moved in before a certain date, then they would PAY YOU $1200.00 to furnish your apartment. PLUS, right after we went through all of that turmoil with the wedding and family, my husband was invited to preach at a service. We had been to this church many times. They were like family to us. On this Sunday, during the altar call, a lady came and put a piece of paper in my hands. At first, I thought it was a note, but when I looked at it, it was a check. I didn't look at the amount, I just said "Thank you, Jesus", and kept working at the altar. After service, I told her thank you, gave her a hug, and proceeded to get in the car. When we got down the road, I remembered that the lady had given me a check, and took it out of my pocket. This woman had handed us a check for $2500.00!!! Oh, and it didn't bounce!!!!

So, within a month of us moving into our place, God had shown HIS grace and favor to us in miraculous ways. How many times have you heard of an apartment complex paying you a check to move in??? Who wouldn't want to serve a God like that???

The God that I serve is definitely one that will let you know when you are in his will. And most times, he will show you in ways that you least expect it, and when you need it the most. The fact that He showed His mercies in a way so miraculously, was what I held on to for years. Whenever I felt like I our marriage wouldn't make it, I relied on the fact that I know what I heard God say, and I saw what He did in our lives.

Psalm 12:2

Ashes No More

A good man obtains favor from the Lord, but a man of wicked devices He condemns.

Ashes No More

Ashes No More

Releasing the residue....Embracing the Strength

Job 13:12

Your memorable sayings are proverbs of ashes (valueless); your defenses are defenses of clay (and will crumble).

I definitely needed that foundation and those memories to fall back on in our marriage. Because the both of us were dealing with so many things from before we met, it caused a lot of problems in the beginning of our marriage. Because of the sexual abuse that I had encountered when I was younger, I had a really big issue with intimacy. The innocence that I had as a child was taken from me, I had no choice in the matter. So, when I got older, I didn't know what intimacy was. And to be honest, it wasn't until I learned what worship was, that I learned what true intimacy was. When I began to spend true time with God, in silence, I learned that it was more than just sex.

Even after I learned what intimacy was, I didn't know how to balance everything. I was not a very sexual person, because I would have flashbacks and I was go to a dark place. I knew that my husband was not the one that did anything to me, but my body and my mind felt differently. There were certain ways that he would touch me that would send me straight back to that place where I had no control….and I would just go numb or start to cry.

I don't think that people really understand how sexual abuse can change someone. Because those things had happened to me years before I met my husband, I didn't think that it would be an issue. Yes, I had talked to my husband about my issues, and we agreed that we would get help and try to find the best ways to deal with it. But, eventually it still caused a big problem.

And after years of dealing with that during my marriage, on top of the other issues that we had, I decided that I just didn't want to deal with it anymore. I didn't want to hold on to those issues anymore. I wanted my husband to be able to touch me and not have to worry about if I was going to slowly pull away, I wanted to be able to trust him wholeheartedly when it came to my body and my emotions. I wanted my *beauty*.

When I got married, I allowed the fear of hurt to have more power than the longing for love that I had been searching for. I didn't even realize how much I had been holding in. I longed for love, but I rejected love when it came. That was a battle within a battle that I was losing daily.

Sometimes, I had to just take a deep breath and try to just take everything in, slowly. During those moments is when I realized just how damaged I had become and just how low my self-esteem was. I had allowed people to just have their way with me for so long, and I had become comfortable with it.

Even being married to my husband. I went through a lot of things in the beginning of our marriage. Even to this day. I always felt like they thought I wasn't good enough to be a part of their family. Though it was not all of his family members, the ones that felt that way definitely let it be known that they did. I had always pictured myself being married and being close to my inlaws. I imagined going shopping with my mother in law and sharing laughs and special moments. I wanted it to feel like a second family. And when I got married and it was nothing like

Ashes No More

that, I was actually mad at God for a long time. I didn't understand why He would put me in that type of situation. Every single relationship that I had been in before I met my husband included me having a wonderful relationship with their parents and families, as a whole. I always looked forward to being around them, and that is what I expected when I got married, too.

It seemed some people in his family found every little reason that they could to not like me. Once, they even got mad at me for sitting next to him and church, because I was not his wife yet. They said that "looked" bad.

Now, I am not writing all of this because I am trying to make his family look bad, but I am writing this because I know that there are some people out there that may be going through the same thing, and you need encouragement. It took a while for my husband to break loose from his family. Not because they were so "close knit", but because he was just one of those people who wanted to please everyone and didn't like for people to be mad at him. He was the one that everybody went to when they needed something done, because they knew that he would do it with no problem. He was the one that they knew they could say anything to, and he wasn't going to get smart in the mouth or give them a hard time. We argued plenty of nights, and he sometimes felt torn, I'm sure. But he eventually realized that he had to take care of home, and

Ashes No More

that meant that their feelings would be hurt sometimes.

The nights that I cried because of the words that were said behind my back, and even the words that were said to my face, I will never forget. Parents used to teach their children to say "Sticks and stones may break my bones, but words will never hurt.". That is an absolute lie. I have endured more pain and needed more healing from the words that have been said to me. Words replay in your mind over and over. And there are some things that I may never forget. But I am definitely praying for deliverance from words. We are sometimes bound because we wont let go of words that were spoken years ago. Yes, sometimes when those words are said to you or even someone close to you, you may feel like you are right back in that moment when it first happened. But we cant allow that to take us back to that place completely and forget all the progress that we've made.

I have had people try to physically fight me during church, I have had people tell me that they never wanted me to be with my husband, and that I was just ugly. I have been told that I was never going to be anything. One of my former Pastors even told my mother that they didn't think that I was going to make it out of college without having a baby.

Ashes No More

Throughout my life, I definitely always felt like it was one things after another. I did feel like I simply was not good enough. I said earlier in this book that I went through a time where I felt like I wasn't even good enough for God. I didn't think that he would have anything that I would be worthy enough to do for Him. The sad thing is that once I got myself together and realized that God could use me *even more* because of the things that I had gone through, people came and made me second guess what I already knew to be true. People came and made me feel like God was not going to be able to use me because of my past. Every time I would have arguments with some people, the first words out of their mouth would be "You ain't nothing but a dyke anyway."

I have come to realize that the church is always so quick to judge the sin, without ever asking what the root was. Sometimes I still deal with having to go back to my home town for things of ministry. Simply because I know that even though people believe in change and strive for it every day, not everyone will receive from me because they know about my past.

It is also my opinion that most hurt people, hurt people. So, I always told myself that I was not going to hurt people the way that some people hurt me, and I wasn't going to put everyone in the category of "people trying to hurt me". I do not want to be that person that is always playing the victim. I am where I am because of all that has happened to me. My goal is to help other people work through the process of healing, and to embrace the strength that they didn't know that they had. I had no idea of the strength that was inside of me. And sometimes when I look at other people my age, I wonder if they would have handled the things that I did, in the manner that I did, still carrying the grace that I am. After years of wondering if things would ever get better, I adjusted into knowing that this is what I was graced for.

In life, we sometimes take for granted the lessons that we have been taught. And it wasn't until I got older that I realized just how rude that is to the teacher of those lessons. Have you ever been in a class, and allowed everything else to distract you from what you should have been learning. The lesson was taught the way that it was supposed to be, and nothing was wrong with the teacher. You just decided to focus on other things and didn't catch the lesson that was being taught. The lesson was taught...but you didn't learn. In school, you have to go through the same lesson again, when you don't get it the first time. And it's the same way in life. The only difference, is that the teacher of life cares unconditionally for you, and won't give up on you.

It was in those times where I didn't know how my next move was going to make a difference, that I had to trust totally and completely on Him.

Ashes No More

I had no other choice. I didn't know when I was going to get passed the hurt and when the tears were going to stop, but I knew that He would get the glory out of it all, and that I had a purpose in this world.

Holding on to things from our past sometimes seems to be comfort. We wonder why, and most times, it is because hurt seems to be the only consistent thing in our lives. It seems to be the only thing that we can expect. But that's not what God wants for us. He wants us to see the hurt, but not to live in it. Have you ever seen someone that seemed to have it altogether meet up with someone or a group of people that seemed to always have issues. Sometimes, after the person that seemed to have it altogether has been around the others for so long, they seem to start having constant issues, as well. And that's what some of us do in life. When God puts us in a place or around a people that we can make a difference and we decide to become a part of the issue, it just makes it harder for us.

Now, let's talk about how we can move on from some things. When I was sexually abused time after time again, I felt dirtier and lower every time. So, I didn't think that I would ever be able to get passed it. But the thing that got me through that time, after I gave my life completely to Christ, was intimacy with God. Spending quality time with him. I am also a lover of music. For three months straight, I watched no television. I only listened to music, read books, prayed, worshipped, and listened for His voice. I am not saying that you have to be super spiritual. I am saying that for me, I knew that I had to shut myself out from the world for a while, and focus on Him.

As women, we don't realize the harm that can come from constant relationships. If you are not married, and you are praying for a husband, learn to love yourself first. I didn't know what love was. Therefore, I didn't know what I was looking….while I was looking. So, even if I had found it, I probably wouldn't have embraced it. People say that you can't miss what you never had, but I beg to differ. That's how you explain the millions of young men missing mother and father figures, and the same with young women.

We, as women, should not depend on the validation of men to feel beautiful. We shouldn't always have to have a man around for them to compliment us and make us feel worth anything. It is in those times of being alone and true intimacy with God, that we are able to see ourselves. If we can't be alone with ourselves, why should we expect any man to want to be?

And sometimes, even during marriage, we become dependent upon hearing the other person tell us sweet things and compliment us, until when we are alone, we don't know how to cope with ourselves. Even in relationships, we have to constantly make time to love on ourselves. If we don't, when things get hectic in life, all it will take is for someone to tell you something nice or sweet for you to be swept off of your feet.

Releasing the ashes of your past will definitely be a process. It will not happen overnight, and every day will not be easy. Sometimes thoughts will come into your mind, and sometimes your emotions may seem more powerful than the process. You just have to keep reminding yourself that this is needed for your sanity.

God's blessings will definitely be proof that you are on the right track. That's how I knew that I was on the right track. Things seemed to begin to fall into place. I began to feel freer than I had ever been.

But, I know that I cannot go into detail about every blessing that I have received, and every trial that ended triumphantly for me. But I just wanted to share a piece of my story to encourage someone else that they can move on. I wanted to encourage someone else to know that they don't have to keep holding on to the ashes. I used to tell my husband that when I died, I wanted to be cremated. I didn't see the point in getting me all dressed up and putting me in a box to be buried under feet of dirt. I told him that I wanted him to keep my ashes and put it somewhere for everyone to see. I wanted him to be reminded of our love on a daily basis.

And there is nothing wrong with keeping the ashes of a loved one. But in most cases, ashes represent mourning. Merriam- Webster Dictionary defines ashes as something that symbolizes grief, repentance, or humiliation. In Isaiah 61:3, the bible talks about giving beauty for ashes. One night, I was reading that scripture, and I heard God say that He wasn't giving beauty in place of ashes, but in exchange for ashes. When something is given in place of something else, it can be replaced with another dead thing. But, He didn't want us to hold on the ashes and have the beauty, too. God wants us to give the ashes to Him. He was us to give the grief and humiliation back to him, so that He can, in turn, give us the beauty. Have you ever been in a relationship, and wanted to help someone, but they didn't want the help? Or maybe it was a family member or friend? You gave them every opportunity to get what they wanted or needed, but you just needed them to free themselves and let you know what it was that they were in need of. That's what God is waiting for us to do. He is just waiting for us to let go of the things that we are holding so tightly to, and give it to Him, so that he can give us the beauty. Why keep the ashes, when they have no use?

I had to learn this lesson, first hand. I had to let go of the ashes from my past. I had to let go of

Ashes No More

the things that I was holding on to in my heart. Just because we don't think about things all the time, doesn't mean that they are not in our hearts. Sometimes we suppress memories and words that have been spoken to and over us, and we don't think that it's an issue. Then, something happens one day and we start having all of these feelings. We can't seem to figure out why we are feeling the way that we are, but we forget about all those things that we never dealt with and that we never gave over to God. That's just like keeping the ashes of a loved one and keeping in a closet or someplace that you will hardly see it. You don't want to get rid of it, because somehow the pain gives you an odd sense of comfort, but you don't want to see it because along with that comfort comes hurt. But then one day, you happen to stumble across the ashes, and every emotion that you could have imagined comes back, all at once.

God is a Father. He doesn't want His children hurting over things that he can help with. Who wants to see their children put themselves through repeated and unnecessary pain?

That's where the prayer of release comes in. We always pray about "Release", but in the sense of Him releasing His power, and His grace. We pray that He releases His peace and His blessings. But sometimes we have to pray that God will help us to "Release" the ashes, so that we can receive.

Ashes No More

So, I pray that in reading this, you have been encouraged to release the residue of your past, and embrace the strength of your overcoming. Let go of the ashes, so that you can flow freely in His beauty. He wants us to deal with the issues of our past no more. He wants us to have ashes…..no more!

Conclusion

With all that had happened to me, I didn't
realize until I got married, just how much of it

Ashes No More

that I actually held on to. I didn't think that I would have so many trust issues to deal with. I didn't think that I would have so many flashbacks and triggers. Furthermore, I didn't think that I had so many walls blocking my emotions. I thought that I had moved passed a lot of things. The way my thinking was set up, I was more than ready to give me all to someone and commit to another person for the rest of my life.

What I didn't know was that the issues that I had were not only going to cause problems in my marriage, but even when it came to things in ministry.

Have you ever been in a place where you simply felt like you were lost? When I got married, and started doing the things that I should have been doing, that's when I saw that things weren't going to be as I envisioned.

I know that not only women will read this book, but I can only speak from a woman's point of view. Therefore, as women, we sometimes tend to hold things in when we feel like our words no longer have power. Some women can scream and yell until there is no end, but after a while....I tend to give up and just shut down. So, after I have shut down in a particular area for so long, I just push it to the back of my mind and act like it never happened. And for a while, that approach worked, in my opinion. I thought that I was handling things correctly, and as long as I wasn't bringing things up and fussing then I was ok.

But the truth is, the silent issues are the deadliest. The ones that we push aside and put away are the ones that cause the most pain when they are revealed again. We treat our issues the same way that some people handle the ashes of a loved one. Normally, people will try to find the most beautiful urn possible to fill with the remains of a person that was once close to them. It is usually placed in an area that is open enough for it to be accessed, if needed…but not in a place that represents a constant reminder of what once was. And we do that same thing with the things that we hold in. We put on the most beautiful mask that we can create and we push the issues far enough in the back of our minds, so that we don't have to deal with them on a regular basis…but we hold on to them, so that we can still have those comfortable, yet painful memories.

And throughout all of it, we don't see that it's hurting us, more than it is helping us. It took me more time than it should have to learn that I need to just be open about my feelings concerning different situations that happened in my life, and realize what the consequences are. Once I have realized what the consequences were, I learned that I have to find ways to not cope with them, but make use of them. The sad

Ashes No More

thing is that we are more comfortable in pain. We are more comfortable in pain, because it seems to have been more faithful to us than anything else. It has been reliable.

That is the reason that I started the ministry of "Ashes No More". I want people to know that we have to be WILLING to EXCHANGE our ashes for the beauty that has been promised to us. Most of God's blessings are "conditional" blessings. Meaning we can have the blessings, on condition of us giving up things....and in this case....it's the ashes of our past that we need to get rid of. He wants us to give them to Him. He wants to give us the beauty that we deserve.

There have been so many things that have been said about me, and I if I said that they didn't bother me, I would not be telling the truth. There have been so many nights that I have cried and asked God what is was about me that people disliked. I even saw myself slowly falling into a depression. I would put on a smile in front of people, and my spirit would be crying out for a renewing and refreshing. I did allow people to control the way I thought about myself, and the way I perceived some things about myself.

When you have someone tell you that you are never going to be anything, and that you are the reason that your husband is "not successful", it can make you question your own actions. I even started blaming myself for some things that I already knew deep down inside was not my fault.

My husband "got on me" plenty of times about allowing people to control my actions and emotions. I had to learn to allow things to be "dealt with", without being held on to.

I had to be the first partaker in Ashes No More. I had to trade in all of the humiliation and embarrassment of my past. The crazy thing is that I never felt bad about my past. I knew that some things were not right, but I also knew that when I gave my life over to Christ, all things became new. I allowed the words of people to push guilt and humiliation onto me. And I held on to it. I embraced it.

Ashes no more is a ministry that helps to Release the Residue, and Embrace the Strength.